My Friend, Holy Spirit

 Written by Monica Sotolongo

Illustrated by Satchel Celeste Causey

Copyright © 2021 Monica Sotolongo.

All rights reserved. This book or any portion thereof may not be reproduced or used in any manner whatsoever without the express written permission of the publisher except for the use of brief quotations in a book review.

Printed by R & J Publishing., in the United States of America.

First printing, 2021.

abidetolove.org

To my Best Friend and the One I love most: Father God, Jesus and sweet Holy Spirit. To my husband, my earthly best friend: I love you forever. To my children: David, Noah, Johanna, Sarabeth, Daniel, Judah, Gracelin and Elijah. Each of you are my treasures. I adore being your mama.

To all of the children and families who will read this book: May you encounter the kindness and friendship of Holy Spirit like never before. I pray you say yes to Him for all of your days!

-Monica

For Mom, and in loving memory of Grandma. Thanks for showing me what selfless love and generosity looks like.

-Satchel

Hi sweet one!

I want to introduce you to my very best friend. His name is **Holy Spirit!** **Holy Spirit** is the Spirit of God.

God the Father,

God the Son, Jesus,

and God the Holy Spirit.

Holy Spirit was there when the Earth was formed.

He saw you when you were growing in your mom's belly.

Holy Spirit knows what time you were born.

He knows your hair color, your eye color, how many toes you have, and all the things that are secret in you!

Holy Spirit knows what you are good at and what you really love to do. He gave you those gifts! He also knows the things that you don't like. He knows what has scared you or what has made you cry.

Holy Spirit is *always* with you.
He never, ever leaves you.

He thinks you are the most special person in the world. He loves you SO much!

Holy Spirit wants to be your friend.

He wants to talk to you all day long.

He also wants to <u>listen</u> to every single thing you want to say to Him.

He wants you to talk to Him when you walk, when you are at school, and when you are laying in your bed at night.

He wants you to talk with Him when you are mad, when you are sad, and when you are excited and happy!

He loves you very much and wants to help you every day.

Holy Spirit wants you to know that anytime you need Him, He is right there with you. He wants you to know that with Him, you don't have to be afraid.

He provides for you when you are hungry and thirsty.

Just come to Him and He will give you what you need.

Holy Spirit wants to take you on adventures with Him, whether you are poor or rich.

He wants you to be His friend and also in His family.

All you need to do is say yes.

When you say yes, He comes in and promises to be with you forever.

Are you ready to say yes?

Remember earlier, when I shared with you that God is 3 in 1? God the Father, God the Son-Jesus, and God- the Holy Spirit?

God the Father sent His Son, Jesus, over 2,000 years ago on a special mission. Jesus came to the Earth so that He could pay the price for every bad thing we have ever done, or will do. Those bad things are called sin. Without this special sacrifice, we cannot be with God, because God is holy. Holy means there is no sin with God. This was a problem, because God wants to be with us every day. So, God the Father had a solution. He sent His Son, Jesus, to pay the price for our sin so that we wouldn't have to. When He died on the cross, the Bible says that He took all of our sins for us. The good news is that after Jesus died, He rose up 3 days later and even defeated death. If we will say yes to this gift, He will give us the free gift of salvation AND send Holy Spirit to come live inside of us.

Romans 10:9 "If you declare with your mouth, "Jesus is Lord", and believe in your heart that God raised Him from the dead, you will be saved."

Ephesians 3:16 "I pray that out of His glorious riches he may strengthen you with power through His Spirit in your inner being."

PRAYER

Heavenly Father,

   Thank you for sending the gift of Holy Spirit to those who give their life to Jesus. I believe Jesus paid the price for my sins when He died on the cross. So right now, I ask Jesus to come and forgive all of the bad things in my heart. I receive Jesus' free gift of salvation AND Holy Spirit into my life. I also know I am now a daughter/son of God, my Heavenly Father. Wherever you lead me, I will follow. I give you my whole life. Thank you for being my Best Friend. **I love you.**

www.ingramcontent.com/pod-product-compliance
Lightning Source LLC
LaVergne TN
LVHW071028070426
835507LV00002B/63